Professional Counselling
Diploma
for
Sexual Abuse

Karen E. Wells

Copyright

Table of Contents

Introduction

Welcome to this professional-level course about counselling for sexual abuse survivors. This course has been designed to provide in-depth information into how to help and support those who have experienced extreme sexual trauma. Sufferers are likely to have a multitude of conflicting issues and these will no doubt, impact on a psychological and physiological level. Abuse can impact every area of life including, social abilities, self-beliefs, career potential and relationships too.

Due to the nature and severity of these traumas, we would advise that you already have some counselling experience or are qualified in psychotherapy so to truly understand the effects of trauma on the mind. If you have not studied counselling previously, we would suggest that you do so alongside this course as this will help you to provide a greater depth of understanding and knowledge to those who come into your care. We do however, provide a great deal of information within these modules that will enable an accurate and comprehensive approach to the complexities of this type of sexual abuse.

If you have plans to become a counsellor specializing in this aspect of trauma, know that you will no doubt hear some harrowing experiences, and these may affect you deeply. Learning how to cope with these occurrences is something that must be learned and developed for your own protection and well-being. There is a balance to be taken between empathy and pure professionalism. We include information about this in the first module so that you can understand the types of issues that you will be facing.

There is no doubt that counselling survivors of sexual abuse will be deeply rewarding once you start to see the changes in your client's lives. Each client will have a unique set of experiences, and these experiences will have shaped the way they are in a unique way. As you work your way through this course, you will understand that your approach must be intuitive and tailored to each client so that you can help them on the road to recovery. Counselling sessions are likely to be for the long term, and you must be prepared to take this on board and offer stability in a world that may seem terrifying and completely out of control.

To aid your understanding of the information given, we provide self-assessment tasks at the end of each module and suggest that you take time to answer the questions or to complete the tasks to ensure your full comprehension of the information given. Please do not submit the self-assessment tasks for review. If you struggle with these assessments, please re-read the module before continuing with the next.

At the end of the course, you will find a final assessment, and this should be completed and sent for review. Please take your time. We encourage due diligence and dedication so that you can feel confident in your role as a counsellor while giving the best help to those who need it.

To be able to help others, you must fully understand the intricacies of sexual abuse and how it affects the mind long after physical traumas have healed. When you are ready, turn to module one.

Module One

Understanding Trauma as A Counsellor

As a counsellor working with complex traumas, you will no doubt encounter those with deeply rooted issues and helping these clients can be very difficult. You will be exposed to cases of dehumanization which can place extensive emotional pressure on you. As a practitioner, helping those who have experienced sexual abuse, you must be very aware that there may well be Primary Traumatic Stress (PTS) or Secondary Traumatic Stress (STS). The symptoms of stress can impact life in varying ways – emotionally, spiritually physically and cognitively. This also includes behaviors. You must look after your own needs and ensure you are resilient creating strong foundations upon which to work and by doing so, it provides a safe space for survivors of abuse. This is important.

We discuss this here because it is important that you understand the implications of this role. Some of the stories that you hear will be harrowing. You will see how the trauma has affected those who come to you for help which can impact how you view human nature and the world around you. Being exposed to the suffering and pain of others can be overwhelming. There may be times when you feel powerless to help those who have experienced such traumas. Counsellors who are exposed to these traumatic situations frequently will specify that they experience strong reactions including:

- Anger

- Disbelief.
- Powerlessness.
- Helplessness.
- Loss of faith.

These types of feelings often coexist and can lead to self-sacrificing behaviors. It's important to note at this point that there is a line between helping those clients who seek your professional advice and becoming overinvolved with them. The opposite can also occur. Sometimes practitioners begin to disengage from those they see due to the level of trauma and this is a defense mechanism. This can occur for a period of time which can lead to STS.

Counsellors must be aware of burnout as it is a very real risk. There is a great deal of pressure on counsellors to help those in their care and much of the pressure will come from within. This is a responsible role and certainly, emotive. Monitor your reactions regularly so to offset any negative impact. You can do this through reflecting on your reactions to any narratives within the sessions.

To avoid developing burnout, it is worth considering the following questions:

- Are you feeling run down or do you find yourself being drained of any physical or emotional energy?
- Do you feel that you are prone to negative thinking when it comes to your job?
- Have you started to be less sympathetic with people that deserve sympathy?
- Have you started becoming irritated by colleagues or when small issues occur?
- Do you feel misunderstood or unappreciated by those you work with?
- Do you feel isolated within your role and that you have no one to talk to?
- Do you feel that you are achieving less than you should be?
- Is there a high level of pressure to succeed?
- Do you feel that you are not gaining what you need from your job?
- Have you started to believe you are in the wrong profession?
- Are there times when certain aspects of your job become frustrating?
- Does bureaucracy play a role in your ability to work well and do you find this frustrating?

- Do you have more work to complete than you are able to do?
- Have you started to contemplate that there is insufficient time to complete the parts of the job that are important?
- Are you unable to plan is much as you would like to?

Secondary traumatic stress

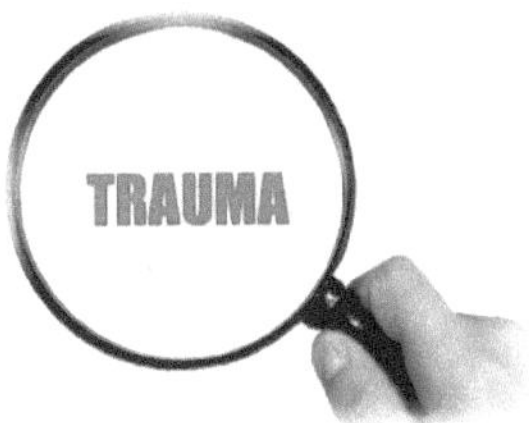

Secondary traumatic stress is often characterized by symptoms relative to those within PTSD. This includes avoidance, arousal and intrusion. Many of the symptoms will be natural reactions to stimuli. However, if you have started to demonstrate some of these symptoms then they must be monitored as they could certainly have a negative impact on life – professionally or personally.

Common reactions

- Trauma-like reactions including numbness, increase physiological arousal, hypervigilance.
- Somatic reactions including exhaustion, nightmares, restlessness, apathy, changes in appetite behaviors.
- Cognitive changes including intrusive thoughts, increased focus on abuse, produce concentration, uncertainty, fragmented assumptions about the world around you.
- Behavioral actions including disconnecting from others, self-medicating, avoidance, being overly or under-protective towards your own children.
- Emotions including feeling powerless, helpless, feeling a sense of despair, losing trust and anxious

It is clear to see that there will be negative implications working with those who have severe trauma. You may find that your behavior alters along with your emotions and in fact, you can experience similar feelings to the responses of the survivor. Understandably, because of the level of sensitive information given over an extensive period, as the therapist, you must become the container, not just for your client but for personal reactions or responses. As such, this can very easily lead to symptoms like PTSD and this should not be ignored.

Some counsellors begin to feel desensitized to the suffering of others, withdrawing from the emotions they experienced as a result and this makes it more difficult for them to feel empathy or compassion for those that they are treating. Where there is secondary traumatic stress, it may even lead to fragmented assumptions about themselves, others or about the world around them. This can add to feelings of anxiety and helplessness.

Certainly, if you start to have trouble sleeping, feel discouraged about your personal future, if you feel jumpy, or find it difficult to concentrate, you could have STS. Other symptoms include wanting to avoid working with some clients, becoming irritated or annoyed, constantly expecting something bad to happen and losing memory.

Some counsellors take on more and more work – this is often to test their own abilities to cope with the pressure although this is on a subconscious basis. Unfortunately, as the counsellor starts to withdraw, there is an even greater sense of feeling helpless, isolated or powerless. Avoiding these types of symptoms and behaviors can lead to more mistakes being made, there may be wrong decisions made and even avoidance of work-related tasks. Some counsellors become too engaged with trying to rescue the survivor or may even develop feelings of blame towards the client for feeling the way they do.

Once you have qualified, it is important that you seek appropriate support if you start to feel fatigue, emotional or, worry that you are suffering from burnout or STS. It is so important to have a good personal support network around you. It is wise to have another counsellor so that you can debunk your feelings.

To be able to understand how your role may impact on you, consider the following signals relative to stress:

Write down the ways that your role impacts on you.
Consider how you know you are feeling stressed and write down any signs or symptoms that are being demonstrated, then consider how you manage the symptoms.
Identify some of the triggers that lead to your becoming stressed and then reflect on all that you've written considering how you could manage the triggers and, your personal stress response.

There are four sources of support as identified by Salzer (2002) including:

- Emotional
- Informational.
- Instrumental
- Companion

If we consider emotional support, this would be the type of support that you gain from your family members, a partner or friends.

- Informational support is where you turn to colleagues, a manager or other professional counsellors for support.
- Instrumental support is a type of support where assistance is required so that you can finish those unpleasant tasks.
- Companion support is the type of support gained through feeling connected to others and these include your interest in life, hobbies or sports.

Self-care is all important when it comes to this counselling those who have experienced sexual abuse or, indeed, any type of abuse. You must be able to express your own vulnerabilities and dependency needs and this will enable you to avoid self-sufficiency or defensive feelings of invisibility.

To offset this, it can help to pursue those pleasures in life that provide the most relaxation or perhaps, indulge in creative pursuits for self-expression. Many therapists who are feeling overwhelmed within their roles, might say that they do not deserve to take the time out and as such can become self-sacrificing.

Try yoga, meditation or activities such as tai chi or martial arts.

Module One

Self-Assessment Tasks

Task:

Consider your motives for studying this course, write down why you wish to embark upon this career choice and your plans for doing so. Making a detailed list of why and how you plan to implement this training into your professional life will be useful in terms of motivation and progression. Refer to it when needed.

Task:

What is STS?

Task:

What sort of emotions might you experience through helping those who have been sexually abused?

Task:

How do you plan to debunk if you have listened to many harrowing stories in the sessions of the day?

Please note that these self-assessment tasks are to ensure your understanding of the information within each module. As such, do not submit them for review with Karen E. Wells.

Module Two

Session Traumas

Each person's reaction to trauma experienced will be unique and it will also depend on many factors including the type of trauma experienced. As a counsellor, you must consider how often the client was abused and for what duration. If the client was in an abusive relationship or has experienced a traumatic situation for an extensive period of time, there can be many issues to contend with.

Note: Consider the client's relationship to the abuser

When you are working with victims of sexual abuse, it is imperative that you help clients to recognize that both physical and psychological reactions are going to be expressed, and even if responses to the trauma are unpleasant or hurtful, they are designed to protect them. To help the clients understand how this works, consider the function of the immune system – which is designed to fight any viruses or bacteria and to keep the body healthy. So, the emotional immune system works the same, it is designed to protect the individual from emotional turmoil.

Some of your clients are likely to experience PTSD after the trauma and could be demonstrating elevated states of anxiety now. As such, it will be easy to trigger off any inner sensitivity alarm system so care must be taken. It is certainly dangerous to do so as it restricts/prevents the client from being able to recognize any real external dangers. They will be unable to deal with any safety factors with any objectivity.

Understanding the alarm system

As a counsellor, you need to help your clients understand their responses to trauma on both a physiological and neurological level. Whenever we face danger, there are primitive biological mechanisms at work, and this is our internal alarm systems which when activated is designed to help us survive. At this time, the brain releases an abundance of neurochemicals into the system kick-starting a complex chain of reactions.

Note; this is designed to protect the individual from harm.

Of course, this inner alarm system cannot prevent emotional pain, trauma or stressors from occurring, but it can soften the blow and enable the individual to deal with the outcome. When the alarm system starts, it acts as an emotional immune system occurring outside of conscious awareness. It is not under the person's control. So, when you consider that your clients will have survived sexual abuse, they must understand that their reactions would have been caused out of conscious control. So, they are not to blame in any way for how they responded. Once they realize this, it can help to reduce any feelings of self-blame, guilt or even shame.

Once the body's alarm system is activated, it sends urgent signals to the brain so to prepare for fight or flight and it also does something else, it gives the option of freezing. Two crucial biological defense systems come into play, i.e. the sympathetic nervous system and the parasympathetic nervous system.

It is the sympathetic nervous system that creates vital energy necessary for fight or flight. The parasympathetic nervous system reduces the metabolic rate slowing down the heart and results in the freeze response.

Within the brain, there are two structures that strive to regulate this alarm system – the amygdala and the hippocampus. These are in the limbic system of the brain. The amygdala has a primary role of detecting any alerts through sound, taste, touch, sight or smell. It is responsible for translating the signals received as to whether a situation is dangerous or non-threatening.

This evaluation occurs in an instant and it does not use a deeper analysis or even, common sense to form a reaction. If the signal is translated as life-threatening, stress hormones are immediately released into the body and this includes adrenaline and cortisol. These send messages through the nervous system to the internal organs and muscles so the individual can fight, run away or, freeze.

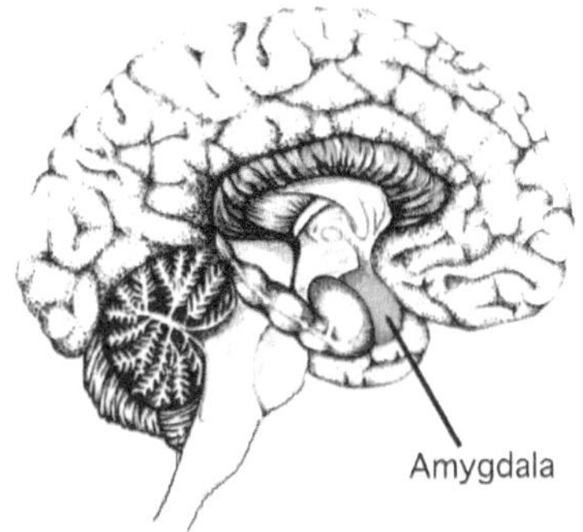

The amygdala is extremely sensitive to any danger and can easily be activated to increase this readiness further. By contrast, the hippocampus takes a slower route in that it evaluates any external threats using conscious thought, memory, reason, logic and so on. This part of the brain is also vital when it comes to laying down new memories and experiences. So, if the danger is very real, the hippocampus sends messages to continue with the appropriate response. If, on a deeper analysis, it suggests the stimuli is not dangerous, then messages are transmitted to deactivate the alerts. Usually, the two structures work in balance so to ensure the right response is made.

However, when prolonged traumas occur and, those that are repeated (complex traumas), it is easy to understand that the two systems of the brain and the feedback loop, can malfunction. When this happens, the body is flooded with high levels of stress hormones. The fight or flight response is natural and critical to survival, but the hormones themselves are highly toxic and damaging if they occur more than for short periods of time.

If you have a client who was sexually abused for a long time, it is likely that the person will have felt trapped and certainly, unsafe which would have led to their freezing, rather than trying to fight back or to escape. In these situations, the stress hormones remain within the body and continue to keep the person on high alert. If the stress response does not dissipate, there can be many negative consequences. Even the brain cells can be distracted, impact the size and function of the hippocampus and the amygdala.

When brain and body are flooded with high levels of stress hormones, the hippocampus cannot evaluate any threats or dangers. As a result, the hippocampus goes off-line. The messages to deactivate the alarm are not received by the amygdala and the stress response assumes that the danger is ongoing. This can lead to the individual feeling that they are constantly being traumatized.

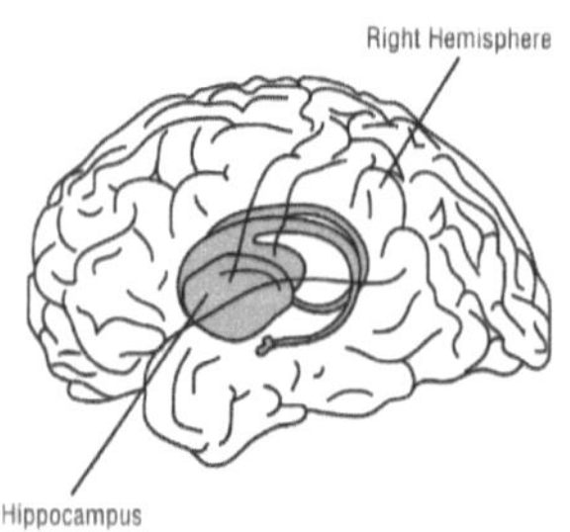

In turn, the hippocampus will be unable to regulate any alarm or prevent chronic levels of stress hormones and will have a reduced ability to store new memories. This means, it becomes difficult or impossible to store the details of the trauma, to process it, or to even add context or time to the memory. This results in the trauma being ongoing which is highly-damaging.

Note: Processing the trauma is absolutely vital for recovery.

Physical health

Where there are high levels of stress hormones for long periods of time, it can lead to physical exhaustion, sleep impairment and respiratory issues. The endocrine system will be impacted along with digestion. Hypertension can also be experienced. The stress response can even reduce the person's ability to process the experience or to reflect upon it. In other words, they cannot make sense of it and so, it continues.

The freeze response

We've mentioned that there are three reactions in the stress response – most commonly, we consider the fight or flight response as it is instinctive to try to run or to fight but, the third option can also be used and that is to freeze. This is used when it is not possible to run or to fight. It is not a flaw and may protect the person from an even worse threat that of brutality. However, in the individual's mind, they may feel that they gave in, and that by doing so, they were passive and perhaps, even to blame. Understandably, even though incorrect, it can make those who survive their traumas feel as if they are to blame for not acting. This can lead to self-blame, guilt and deep levels of shame.

When an adult faces an impossible abusive situation, submitting to the situation (freezing) may be the only option for them.

Their inaction may even continue to haunt them and lead to feelings of deep shame. Ultimately, when someone has overpowered them or held absolute authority over them, it merely heightens their sense of vulnerability

While freezing can have a negative emotional impact, it can protect them from experiencing the full emotional or physical pain. When the parasympathetic nervous system starts, the individual may mention feeling a sense of calmness washing over them, even numbing the body. This may create barriers against the pain, in effect, cushioning it and reduces the understanding of the emotional terror of that trauma.

Once the actual danger is over, these reactions tend to fade, and the stress hormones will be alleviated due to movement.

When there are complex traumas, and no way out, the stress hormones do not discharge but continue within the body increasing any sense of disassociation and numbness. As a result, you will see clients where terror and distress never really fade. This can grow stronger over time as a result leading to greater distress although the mind gradually blocks out the sensation of pain through disassociation and avoidance.

No doubt you will see some clients who suffer from or who demonstrate the symptoms of post-traumatic stress disorder (PTSD), so, it is wise to consider the types of symptoms that can occur:

- Intrusion symptoms - distressing memories and dreams, flashbacks, psychological distress.
- Avoidance symptoms - avoiding thoughts, feelings or distressing memories, avoidance of external reminders i.e. conversations, activities, places, people or objects and avoidance of any feelings interconnected with the traumatic event.
- Alterations in cognition and mood – negative emotions i.e. fear, anger, guilt, shame or horror feelings of detachment and an inability to expend positive emotions and dissociative amnesia.

- Alterations in arousal and reactivity - aggressive behavior or irritable, self-destructive behavior, sleep disturbance, problems with concentration.

Hyperarousal

This is where the client is in a constant state of alert due to heightened levels of stress and hormones, including cortisone and adrenaline. When the body is flooded with stress hormones, there will be anxiety, irritability, restlessness and an inability to control emotions. Adrenaline leads onto palpitations, elevated heart rate and sweating. There may be intense feelings of anger or inner rage.

Make sure that your clients understand that within this state, their alarm system is on an automatic faulty setting so that all the focus and energy is on their stress response and survival. This naturally makes it much harder for them to think clearly and to be able to identify and interpret both internal and external clues accurately.

It can be deemed that those in a hyperarousal state, their reactions are out of control and this includes both negative and positive experiences. In hyperarousal, sleep is also disrupted along with eating patterns and rest. In fact, you may see clients who are so stressed that they just cannot sleep or eat. This of course, leads to additional problems including fatigue. Being in this state can become so normal and your client may not even be aware of its impact.

Hypervigilance

Hypervigilance is the primary symptom of hyperarousal and is where the client is unable to relax or to let their barriers down. These are individuals who continuously anticipate risks or threats in life and monitor their environment for signs of danger.

Avoidance

Some trauma survivors seemingly manage their dire experiences through avoidance. This prevents them from going to certain places, or to indulge in certain activities, they may even feel the need to avoid certain people. They can easily become very isolated. When practicing avoidance, it can also eradicate thoughts and feelings through dissociation and numbing.

If a client tells you they watch a lot of television, or they work hard and for long hours, or, they say they suffer from compulsive behaviors, they may be practicing avoidance which is a method of escape. In the same way that some clients turn to alcohol or drugs, some, indulge with food or self-harming. Know that avoidance only works on a short-term basis – so over-eating will satisfy an inner need for comfort but afterwards, there will be feelings of guilt.

Flashbacks

If the client experiences flashbacks, know that these are intense and disturbing. This is because the experience has not been processed fully or integrated into their memory banks. Because these are so intense, they can be overwhelming and cause an activation of the stress hormones and biochemicals. This acts in the same way as the original trauma. The individual finds themselves sweating, or, experiencing muscular tension and their heart will start to pound and breathing, becomes rapid.

Due to the potency of the flashback, clients may find that they adopt the same posture and mechanisms used during the abusive experience – being submissive or cowering etc.

Note: It is important to understand that flashbacks are merely normal reactions and by no means that the individual is losing control or losing their mind.

When the flashback occurs, the client must understand that this is not the abuse happening over again although it may run through the mind like a cruel replay. It just relates to the experience; the past event is in the past. Sensory stimuli including images, touch, taste, smell, sight and sound can trigger flashbacks.

Nightmares and vivid dreams

Nightmares symbolize the emotional aspects of any experience including anger, humiliation and shame. They're very similar to flashbacks because they represent the unprocessed aspects of the experience. During the dream stage, scenarios unfold so to sort through the trauma, and in many ways, this can be worse for the client. During sleep, the coping strategies that exist go offline and this makes it harder to manage the traumas that occur within the nightmares. However, if the traumas remain unprocessed, these are going to simply keep recurring leading to that individual being unable to sleep.

It can be useful for those who are suffering from vivid dreams and nightmares relating to the traumas, to keep a dream diary and this helps the processing of the trauma while improving overall sleep patterns.

Panic attacks

Panic attacks occur when an individual experiences intense anxiety which can be triggered by any situation. It is frightening. Even the panic attacks that occur without warning can be so severe that they prevent the person from going out or participating in social events. Panic attacks cause breath to be shallow, irregular with a pounding heartbeat and there may be pain and tightness in the chest. The individual may feel as if they are having a heart attack. They will feel trembly, dizzy and even, unsteady on their feet. Some worry that they will faint because they feel lightheaded and may be terrified that they are going to die. Their hands and feet may tingle and there will be an overwhelming desire to run away.

Intrusive memories

Memory is a vital aid when it comes survival because it stores all experiences whether good or bad. We process experiences by viewing them and we elaborate and link them to associated experiences. When we do this, it enables them to be stored as memories which will then be used to govern future behaviors. Through the processing of experiences, it makes them less fearful. If memories are unprocessed, then, it is more difficult to store them away in the memory banks as they still need attention.

These memories can be so distressing that clients will instinctively want to avoid them, but this only makes them even more frightening to deal with. They are also likely to recur more frequently, even if people try not to think about the memories. When they are suppressed, they will still rise to the surface.

In hyperarousal, emotional situations which lead to intense, negative or positive feelings tend to be avoided. This is an automatic response which is governed by the parasympathetic nervous system (where the heart rate and breathing rate slows and the tones of the muscles start to soften, going limp and mind and body, seem to collapse in on itself).

You may find that people go into an almost trancelike state.

Due to this sense of detachment and feeling of numbness, it can be very difficult for the individual to reflect upon those experiences, to process them, or even to feel a sense of compassion for others, let alone themselves.

Disassociation

Disassociation can be deemed a mental flight which occurs because physical flight is just not possible. (Cleft hyper). This is an adaptive response when trauma is deemed inescapable. It provides a barrier of the mind and this enables the individual to detach from anybody's sensations, feelings or, indeed, reality. Once your clients start to understand the type of trauma and of course, the stress reactions, they begin to normalize the symptoms rather than to feel as if they are damaged beyond repair.

Module Two

Self-Assessment Tasks

Task:

How do panic attacks affect individuals?

Task:

What is hypervigilance?

Task:

What is the alarm system?

Task:

Why are nightmares and dreams important when traumas have been experienced?

Task:

Specify your understanding of avoidance.

Please note that these self-assessment tasks are to ensure your understanding of the information within each module. As such, do not submit them for review with Karen E. Wells.

Module Three

Dissociation

Dissociation occurs when someone is facing a situation in which they cannot escape on a physical level, and so, instead, they escape psychologically. They switch off from the experience and the sensations and this includes any thoughts, feelings and their memories too. In addition, that individual person can tune out from the world around them. So, it may even feel unreal to them. In terms of physical experiences, the individual may report that they are floating, looking down at themselves, feeling detached and even, that their body had been separated from the other parts.

There may be huge lapses in memory too, because the mind will blank out part or all the experience and any associated memories can be lost. This can be deemed a normal response to traumatic circumstances but know that it can impact on daily life and over time, it can lead to changes in that person's sense of being and affect their reality too.

It can be so severe that they lose contact with their physical body, or, spend much time lost in their mind, but this can make it very difficult to monitor any actual dangers around them, or indeed, access internal signals to ascertain if something is not right. When detachment is frequent, this can lead to a loss of reality and uncertainty. While this may aid the survival process, at least in the first instance, it can also develop into avoidance of feelings – making them unresponsive even to feelings that are pleasurable.

Dissociation takes a huge amount of energy and can be draining as there will be a lack of emotional context, it can seem as if individuals are cold and even, unfeeling. They will struggle to connect with others, and this will limit or reduce their ability to develop loving relationships. As such, they are wrapped in a bubble of traumatic loneliness. Clients who experience dissociation must understand its nature and, identify the dangers. This is not easy to do.

Dissociation spectrum

We all disassociate to a certain degree – this may be a daydream, we become lost in our thoughts, or in the pages of a good book, and at this point, we become unaware of anything else. This is a normal aspect of detachment from reality. Dissociation is usually found in children and it manifests through their fantasy and imaginings. Due to traumas, some children continue to live in a fantasy world because there is often a need to escape. As such, these are more likely to slip into dissociative imagination.

Ongoing disassociation

While most people will experience detachment and periods of alertness during the day, this will vary and will be dependent on energy levels alongside the chosen activities. Normally, a day will consist of some down times….and there may be some activities that occur on autopilot. This is called automaticity and is where well-practiced activities along with repetitive ones occur outside of conscious awareness.

Within clinical dissociation, detachment can be extreme, and the person becomes lost in the bubble of their own internal world. Their grip with reality is reduced gradually and they could lose their sense of self for long periods of time. This is known is dissociative amnesia. You may find that many of your clients will be unable to recognize dissociative symptoms or struggle to find the words to describe their feelings:

They may say that they feel fragmented or feel as if they are falling apart or floating between sanity and insanity. Your clients may feel as if they're going crazy. Others will say that it feels as if they are separate parts of themselves, and some may even hear voices.

These feelings prevent them from being able to organize their experiences as a whole and because this, therapeutic work is needed so to create awareness of disassociation so that the symptoms. they are experiencing can be brought into the light. Clients need to reflect on their experiences and to verbalize them. This is an important aspect of their being able to make sense of them.

There are various types of dissociation when it comes trauma:

- Primary dissociation happens when there is an overwhelming threat and it stops the individual from integrating this event so that the experience remains fractured.
- Secondary or peritraumatic dissociation occurs when there is no escape from the trauma. As a result, this experience becomes trapped in the right brain and the left-brain can is unable to process it or analyze it.

The most common type of dissociation is known as structural dissociation and it occurs in survivors where the complex trauma is split vertically in the conscious mind and it happens so they can protect themselves against overwhelming fear.

Some survivors with either the primary or secondary structural dissociation can still function at a remarkably high level and they may even have very successful careers, yet, their personal relationships tell a very different story. This may seem very confusing because it is so different to the success they experience in their careers. When you have a high functioning client, they will want to understand why their intimate relationships tend to have so many difficulties. Often, they practice avoidance in their relationships, there may be a fear of intimacy, dependency or a fear of abandonment. The attachment style is split and the 'apparently normal personality' (ANP) detaches and there is no contact with the trauma-related side. At the same time, the emotional personality (EP) remains deeply embedded and lost within the trauma. So, within the primary structural dissociation, the ANP continues to be functional and manages work life and social interactions extremely well, even though on an emotional and physical level, they often feel completely numb.

The emotional personality has to constantly relive the trauma going through post-traumatic symptoms including flashbacks, amnesia and disorientation.

Clients are often unaware that this is happening and to unlock such complex traumas, the survivor must become aware of what is known as inner experiencing and be able to not only tolerate but to be able to regulate it. This is the only way change can be facilitated. As such, they must experience the full intensity of the feelings which will probably include:

- Anger
- Disgust
- Shame
- Sadness.
- Rage

This can be an intense and disturbing process where the clients feel so overwhelmed by these horrifying sensations that they may have trouble breathing and may experience palpitations. Survivors often adopt many avoidance strategies that can support their high functioning lives, but this will not solve the issues.

These are the clients who potentially continue to live in their heads, rather than inhabiting the physical body. They work so hard, so they don't have to examine their feelings and they just keep themselves busy. They may withdraw completely from others and refuse any type of intimacy-this is so that their inner feelings are not experienced. They may practice obsessive compulsive behaviors as this helps them to feel more in control. Those clients who do not function as well, will often resort to alcohol or drugs so to block out any feelings. Some clients may create a parallel world so that this enables the ANP to be able to function. This is often a beautiful and harmonious fantasy world, created just so they can escape their real world. By escaping into this internal world, it can help with post-traumatic growth, however, the downside is that they can become obsessive and addictive about it and less likely to want to come back into reality.

Associated disorders

Where there are severe and chronic dissociation, it is common to discover a range of associated disorders. These can manifest as physical illnesses i.e. aches and pains in the body and no actual reason as to why. Psychological pain will also manifest as aches and pains – in fact, anything from a sore throat through to pelvic pain. Not all your clients will be aware of how dissociation impacts them and so, you need to understand these conditions, so that you can help your client.

Exercise

Identifying dissociative symptoms checklist. Ask your client to fill in these responses.

- Sense of fragmentation.
- Alienation from self/not feeling real.
- Alienation from their surroundings.
- Experiencing too little loss of function.
- Loss of time
- Hearing thoughts or voices that are not their own
- Out of body experiences
- Amnesia.
- Emotions or thoughts that appear out of the blue

Dissociation cues

If you see the following cues when treating a client, they are likely to be dissociating:

- Facial features-glazed look, zoning out, eyes unfocused.
- Inability to speak about the trauma- there may be prolonged silences, they may practice avoidance, helplessness – numb with terror.
- Robotic language-repetitive details.
- Monologues-these are long monologues with a steady stream of consciousness - without any reflection or contemplation.
- Changes in narrative - disorganized and incoherent.
- Misinterpretation - miscommunication.
- Somatic queues - changes in temperature, freezing, physical movements becoming jerky

In addition, you may find that the client has a loss of memory, or, that memory is partial. There may be no recollection of events or even of meeting familiar people or of conversations. They may lose hours or days at a time and find themselves in places where they have no awareness of how they got there.

Module Three

Self-Assessment Tasks

Task:

Explain your understanding of dissociation in full

Please note that these self-assessment tasks are to ensure your understanding of the information within each module. As such, do not submit them for review with Karen E. Wells.

Module Four

Attachment

In this module, we explore the complex traumas further and those pertaining to attachment and worth within a relationship. As a counsellor, you must understand how these issues would impact any future relationships and of course, look at how these traumas could lead to bonding within a relationship while also increasing dependency. We must also consider how trust and the betrayal of it can create a series of difficulties within any relationship and this includes avoidance, attachment and of course, intimacy.

When we talk about attachment, we often consider faulty behaviors within relationships. However, for the survival of the human race, we must consider the bonds which are created from birth and how these attachment bonds are vital for the child's development. These ensure healthy psychological development throughout life and provide the foundations on which all needs, i.e. physical and emotional needs are obtained.

The primary caregiver forms the regulating system that facilitates the child's inner regulation of both arousal and emotional inner psychological mental states. Simply, it provides the regulation of affect while promoting learning so to comprehend experiences, feelings and mental state. These then influence behavior and emotional interaction. Where consistent nurturing is given, the child learns that any distressing emotions can be soothed and regulated. This breeds trust, knowing that others can be relied upon to help them when it is needed. The bonding process releases hormones, including vasopressin and oxytocin, and these are critical hormones which serve to mediate pleasure, delight and comfort all of which are experienced through having a close relationship.

However, if the care given during those early years is either absent or abusive, and at the very least, unpredictable, that young child will not be able to predict the essentials of life accurately and this can lead to a lack of trust in others and even, fear. It will also increase the stress response. In some cases, a child can develop self-sufficiency or others will become over-dependent. Autoregulation can be excessive

Consider that the bonds of attachment help with the regulation of emotions. From this, we can deme that a young child learns how the unbearable aspects of life can be managed. A nurturing environment enables them to understand and trust that their emotional states are soothed by their caregivers and in time, they develop and can self-soothe. Once they can manage emotional states, they can more easily reflect upon and, integrate their emotions and experiences and can learn from them. This leads to the development of empathy for self and for others. They have the necessary skills to be able to function socially and emotionally. This way of being forms the correct balance between being independent and dependent.

Where complex traumas occur during childhood, an individual is not able to feel safe or comfortable around others and of course, this disrupts the attachment system leading to insecure attachments so they either become very dependent on others or the opposite, become independent. So, early attachment styles will have a direct influence on their worth and ability to form positive relationships throughout their lives. When this happens, every relationship can be deemed dangerous or fearful.

When you are treating your clients, you may have to slowly peel back the layers and look beyond the abuse to consider whether there might have been a disruption within their attachment bonds when young. This will not always be the case, but it can lead to insecure, abusive, unloving relationships.

It is worth considering the following:

- Ask the client to provide five adjectives that would describe their relationships with their primary caregiver when young.
- Ask them to recall memories that would support each of these objectives.
- The client should consider how they were able to seek comfort and nurturing during those times of illness or if they were frightened and upset.
- They must consider how their primary attachment figures responded during those times.
- Consider whether they had any separation or losses in early life.
- They should recall if they were ever threatened to be sent away or abandoned even if this was said in a joking manner?
- Did the client experience any sexual abuse during their childhood years, or did they experience any emotional or physical abuse during those times? If yes, why does the client think this occurred?
- If yes, how has that specific relationship developed over time?

You may find that you have clients who find it difficult to recall aspects of their childhood and suffer from fragmented memories or from dissociative amnesia. You can use non-verbal ways of identifying any attachment relationships……asking the client to draw circles that represent themselves and any significant others and the placement of these can be quite telling.

Note that there are five primary adult attachment styles:

- Secure attachment
- Anxious preoccupied.
- Dismissive avoidance.
- Fearful avoidance.
- Disorganized/disorientated/dissociated

If we look at secure attachment, we can connect it to positive, warm and responsive relationships which were consistent throughout childhood into adulthood. This leads to the client developing a positive view of themselves, of others and leads into positive relationships too. These people find it far easier to be close to others in an emotional sense, and they do not worry about being alone or about depending on others or having others depend on them.

Anyone with an insecure attachment style will usually report a lack of support or an unpredictable or emotionally unavailable relationship within childhood leading into adulthood. Because there would have been inconsistency of nurturing, or a direct lack of response to their needs, this would not have regulated the mental state and lead to an inability to trust others and they may expect their partners to be unpredictable, absent or unavailable to them.

Where aversive childhood experiences existed, this can include emotional, sexual violence, neglect or rejection and going forward, the adult would be likely to develop disorganized/disorientated/dissociated attachment styles. This attachment style often fits complex traumas which may have happened in childhood but also, in adult life, and this means the individual may practice avoidance.

In a relationship, there is a complex connection where that person becomes the safe haven but also, the source of fear. So, relationships can be paradoxical and even terrifying, and dissociation becomes their only form of escape. Equally, either the child or the adult is unable to form a sense of self and may have organized attachment strategy.

Complex trauma and attachment

For any survivor of complex trauma, there is often the possibility of that individual not being able to seek comfort from the person who becomes the attachment figure because they are also the abuser. This simply reinforces feelings of isolation and, of course, terror. Each person who survives these complex traumas are likely to react differently to their experiences, but it is common to develop one of the insecure attachment styles. There may also be a distortion of reality, they may favor secrecy too but, it is easy for someone who is abused to develop traumatic bonding with the person who has abused them.

When it comes to traumatic bonding, we can describe it being strong emotional ties that exist between two people, however, one of these people will be abusive, threatening, or may interrogate the other on an intermittent basis. This creates a fearful dependency along with the denial of rage within the person who is victimized. The core features of traumatic bonding are that the person who abuses becomes the person who can also protect and preserve their life, but, like the flick of a switch, this person can also destroy it.

As such, the victim of the scenario will not be able to feel anger or rage because this could lead to further danger and so, these deep emotions must be denied. In this type of relationship, it is plain to see an imbalance of power and one person controls the other. It is worth noting here that the abuse is usually intermittent and exists alongside caring or nurturing. This inconsistency dips into negative and aversive behaviors. To survive the abusive sessions, the victim must distort reality which helps them to overcome the reality of the relationship but by doing so, it normalizes the behaviors of that person.

Equally, the victim becomes more tolerant of the abuse.

Unfortunately, the bond between the victim and abuse can be incredibly strong. So even during therapy, you will find that change is often resisted.

In many cases, the victim starts to identify with the abuser which leads to alterations of perception and cognitive distortion. This can lead to a fear of intimacy or being close to someone, as well as to be fearful of depending on others. There is often a fear of rejection or of being abandoned too.

For fear of attachment and dependency, this usually manifests as being excessively dependent or excessively independent.

During times when healthy dependency needs are not met, you will find that some clients will have sought nurturing through trying to develop relationships just to bring some comfort into their lives. When forced into this type of relationship, the quality of the relationship is not assessed usually because the client will deem that it is better to be in a relationship than to not be in one. This is not the case of course. You may find that some clients will become more compliant or even submissive just to preserve the sanctity of the relationship while other clients may try to gain greater control to keep the relationship intact. This is often seen in domestic abuse.

When dependency needs are not provided, they are often expressed through counter-dependency and this is where one the survivor has had to become self-sufficient and independent. Some clients may have started to deny their own needs, and this can quickly develop into an avoidance of attachment or attachment loss on an almost phobic level.

Two significant fear responses have been identified when it comes to attachment – phobia of attachment is the first and this is where there is a serious aversion to becoming too emotional or too physically close to another person. The second is known as the phobia of attachment loss which is where an intense fear or even panic about losing the relationship starts to manifest. Both fear responses are born from having a desperate need for a loving connection and lead to feelings of shame for having those needs or, through a chronic fear of dependency needs. (Steele and Van der Hart-2009)

Your clients may switch between the two reactions and this can create the thing that they fear the most – conflict and chaos. This sends out mixed messages of course and can make others reluctant to connect. It also reinforces the client's fears so many people end up feeling isolated and alone.

As a counsellor, you need to provide a secure base on which to offer relational regulation so that clients can learn the skills to self-regulate.

Being respectful and accepting of others as well as self.

Having a balance between the co-dependency and being independent.

Being able to set healthy boundaries.

Being warm, engaging, human and genuine

Being emotionally available to themselves as well as to others

Being authentic, non-judgmental and honest

Having empathy

Being able to connect to themselves as well as to others

Being able to reflect

Being able to cope with uncertainty

Traumatic loneliness

Where complex trauma has existed, it often leaves a legacy of needing to override any deep need for connection and instead, it associates with fear and abuse rather than with protection or safety. As you can imagine, if the relationship has developed into a source of conflict and stress rather than being one of pleasure, it is hardly a surprise when you see clients have chosen to withdraw or disconnect from them.

However, this disconnection can lead to a serious sense of isolation and makes them feel alone at times when they most need a connection. Even being surrounded by others will not detract from their innate sense of loneliness. Sadly, those who survived complex traumas have learned that people are not always a source of comfort and that they are much safer when they are alone. This is especially so during the aftermath of any abusive episodes.

> *Being alone can afford a sense of relief and this becomes conditioned within. Rather than reaching out for help and support, it's safer to just hide away, almost becoming visible.*

There is logic in this because your clients may have learned that when visible, it can lead to more abuse and yet when they are quiet, or alone, they are safe.

The sense of loneliness can alter perception, thoughts, feelings as well as expectations and will reduce the potential for them to develop the necessary social skills so to be able to establish and of course, maintain positive relationships.

As a counsellor, you need to be fully aware of how pervasive this loneliness is and to monitor those elements that serve to maintain the sense of withdrawal or isolation.

Factors that maintain traumatic loneliness include:

- Safety in being alone.
- Mistrust and fear of others.
- The need for invisibility.
- Distorted perceptions, expectations, emotions and predictions etc.
- Feelings of shame over dependency – retreating into isolation and gaining a sense of safety.
- Having a lack of healthy boundaries.
- Aggression directed towards self and others for self-protection.
- Where relationships become exhausting, complicated or frightening rather than being supportive or pleasurable.
- A lack of ability to make friends and to develop connections.

Entering into therapy can be hugely difficult for those who have endured sexual abuse or indeed, any type of trauma. The recovery process can be as daunting as anything else. Those people who do become clients may develop a fear even of being too close to you as their therapist or, worry about becoming dependent on you. As such, they could reject any attempt to establish a therapeutic alliance.

Module Four

Self-Assessment Tasks

Task:

What is meant by traumatic loneliness?

Task:

Why might a client reject attempts at creating a therapeutic alliance?

Please note that these self-assessment tasks are to ensure your understanding of the information within each module. As such, do not submit them for review with Karen E. Wells.

Module Five

Trauma Therapy

As a counsellor, it is important that you can build a safe environment for your clients so that you can unlock these difficult experiences so to aid their recovery. This means, understanding the basic principles of trauma therapy. Many of your clients are likely to have experienced dehumanization when sexually abused and your goal is to help reverse this.

Building rapport with your clients can take time. It can be slow going where clients gradually start to trust you sufficiently so to navigate through their difficult experiences. Once trust is established, you can help your clients to reconnect with their inner worth building on the foundations of change and eventually, this helps them to connect to others without having that inner fear they might be abused again.

Within this model, we look at the principles of trauma therapy, highlighting the importance of assessing progress and you can use the scales of assessment to assess and measure dissociative symptoms along with PTSD. Psychoeducation is critical when preparing survivors of sexual abuse for the recovery process. It enables them to gain control over their recovery and healing.

Psychoeducation is an evidence-based therapeutic intervention for patients and their loved ones that provides information and support to better understand and cope with illness

On a behavioral level, psychoeducation deals with perceptions, emotions, relaxation, self-care and coping mechanisms. It is designed to provide knowledge about the condition that exists. There are various stages, and all must be included for it to be psychoeducation. It is a useful method of helping the client to understand what has happened to them and why they feel the way they do.

Psychoeducation is psychotherapy with education.

Connecting to self

Within each session, there is much to be aware of. Understandably, some clients will need more time than others so, try to factor in the anticipated length of the session and how to pace it. Consider any boundaries too which could impact the whole process. Sometimes, it is a case of one step forward and two back. Control dynamics and power must also be considered. The focus will always be on safety, stabilization and ensuring the acquisition of skills prior to starting any narrative.

To enable the client to reconnect with self…consider core therapeutic goals.

- Safety and stabilization
- Create secure foundations.
- Re-establish control over any trauma response.
- Create reflection and mindfulness.
- Psychoeducation and normalization symptoms.
- Validate existing coping skills.
- Process traumatic experiences
- Restoration of reality.
- Challenge distorted perceptions.
- Rebuilding relational worth through the therapeutic relationship.
- Making sense of traumatic experiences.
- Reconnecting to self.
- Reconnecting to others in the world around you.

- Grieving losses.
- Restoring autonomy and self-efficiency.
- Post-traumatic growth.

Remember that each of your clients will be unique when it comes to their personal needs so you must build this into the recovery program and ensure you are able to commit fully. Clients need stability and consistency. Let your clients know that they have your complete focus and attention and you can go at their pace. When they start to relax in the sessions, you can make some headway.

Assessment

It is vital to include an assessment when it comes to post-traumatic stress symptoms and by assessing, it will enable you to identify any primary and secondary symptoms as well as any relative disorders.

When we talk of primary symptoms, we mean the trauma reactions instigated because of the trauma. Secondary symptoms are the attempts made by your clients to manage the primary impact and include:

- Self-harming
- Self-medicating
- Substance abuse
- Withdrawing

As time goes on, those secondary symptoms could lead to dissociated disorders including:

- Substance dependency
- Chronic depression
- Personality disorders
- Self-destructive behaviors

You must assess the primary and secondary symptoms so to provide the appropriate therapeutic modalities.

In the main, survivors of these types of traumas, and those who have been dehumanized usually benefit from experiencing a warm and engaged relationship, so it is best to aim for this rather than a clinical one. Of course, this can be difficult because you are governed by standardized protocols. It is important to balance the needs of the client along with professional assessments.

Anyone who has survived the trauma of sexual abuse should be considered strong and resilient even if they do not feel this way. Each person will have their unique needs and will not fit into a set category. Do not rush the client's progress. If there are deeply rooted and unresolved fears, this can simply make them retreat. They may also feel inadequate if they are unable to go at the pace you set for them. By controlling the session too much, it can reactive the dynamics of abuse as they will feel that their life is being governed by someone more powerful or in control.

As a counsellor, you must be mindful of how to use assessment scales, there are many different forms available and you can use self-administered checklists or a questionnaire. You can also ask questions on an informal basis. This helps make it feel less rigid. Ultimately, it is about your ability to gain access to those deeply rooted memories or concerns and to get to know your clients.

Notice that some of your clients may not reveal complex traumas or even dissociative disorders until later in the process of recovery. At these times, assessment scales may be used if you wish to form a generalized assessment.

Dissociating

A great many of your clients are likely to dissociate and it can be useful to have some simple questions ready so to identify dissociative symptoms. It is worth assessing clients in various ways throughout therapy treatment and this will enable you to keep track on any symptoms or issues as they start to ask the clients what they need or what would be helpful in the therapeutic process and what would be least helpful. This opens communication while reducing the power dynamic.

This is empowering as they can start to take ownership of their own recovery and healing – with your help of course. Both you and your client will need to review their learning and to ascertain skills keeping in mind the therapeutic goals. You may decide to hold group therapy sessions or continue sessions on an individual basis.

Psychoeducation

We have mentioned this before, but psychoeducation is a very important part of the whole healing and recovery process as each sufferer must be able to make sense of their experiences and reactions. It involves the sharing of information so to improve awareness and, to improve cognitive understanding.

Once your clients have knowledge about how the trauma has impacted them and they can understand the recovery process, it will be possible for them to develop reflective function and metacognition. This in turn, enables them to understand their experiences more. In other words, they can make sense of it.

This leads to the normalization of their reactions and helps clients to take more control, rather than being overwhelmed by emotions. This helps to create some control over what may seem like chaos in their lives. Knowledge and reflections help to stabilize trauma reactions, enabling them to develop the necessary skills to have greater choice and control over their responses.

You must be mindful of how knowledge is given because it is important to not overwhelm your clients or to patronize them. You must be intuitive and instinctive when it comes to this, giving the information at the right time for each client. Never lecture the client, but rather express the importance of being able to share information. The session needs to be a two-way thing.

You can ask clients whether they are ready for information so to help them progress, taking control and if they say yes, then, you can discuss more about their situation. Little and often is best. Make sure each session and the recovery processes are carefully paced and keep the tone friendly rather than being all-knowing or acting as an expert because this can trigger the power dynamic.

Think carefully about how to facilitate learning and how the client is likely to consolidate the information given. It needs to be in a way that they can take this information away – perhaps to read and inwardly absorbed. It may be that they have to read the information more than once so that they can reflect upon it. For those clients who are dissociative, this would be more likely. When you consider presenting any information, establish the client's learning style and whether it should be in written form, auditory form or it or involve verbal instruction. You may also want to utilize self-discovery or practical exercises.

Ultimately, you need to find ways to help your clients progress.

Psychoeducation tips

- Verbal instruction.
- Handouts detailing trauma symptoms, which include breathing exercises and techniques on grounding.
- Reading of related books, articles and first-hand accounts.
- Audio files.
- Experiential exercises.
- Documentaries
- Homework-exercises, and keeping a journal
- Skills-base courses including social skills training or assertion training.

If you have any clients who are dissociative, know that they will often switch between the dissociative state and conscious awareness. This means they will find it difficult to receive information and to process and store information. If information is difficult to take in, you will notice the client start to tune out.

You may find that some clients do not even remember receiving some information and of course, when this happens, it will slow down the learning process. If this happens, you must be patient. When you have given out information, check later to see if it was absorbed.

You can do this through:

- Conversation
- Providing homework

Psychoeducation is often used in the early stages of therapy, but it can be ongoing. Exploring the full extent of the trauma experienced is vital and can take time. Some of the clients will gain comfort just by having someone with them. They may struggle to speak. Information gleaned can be slow. Much of the session will involve listening and prompting the client. Learn to use open questions beginning with the following so that the client must open and answer.

- Why?
- What?
- How?
- Who?
- Where?

Do not bombard them with questions but as they open and talk, really listen. You must discuss how you wish to capture the essence of the session. Some clients will not want the sessions to be recorded and some may even struggle with your taking notes. Discussion on this is important. Keep the session flowing. Let the client control the pace. As you discuss recovery, you will set the foundations of change. Psychoeducation should include information relating to the difficulties that the client is experiencing:

- Self-harm
- Self-medicating
- Aspects of their sexuality
- Feeling shameful etc.

There are a variety of factors to consider when working with clients who have experienced severe sexual trauma. Once you have built rapport and trust with each in turn, understand the various layers of trauma which can include their sense of betrayal, physical pain, guilt, shame, self-hatred and so on. Your role is to provide a genuine presence so that the client can actively participate. By developing that human relationship, it is possible for the dehumanizing effects to be reversed.

Important areas in psychoeducation

- The type of trauma, the impact, the symptoms experienced, role of dissociation, role of attachment.
- The recovery process and post-traumatic growth.
- The therapeutic process-therapeutic goals, contracts, duration phase-orientated treatment and the nature of therapy.
- The role of collaboration within the therapeutic relationship.
- Trauma symptoms-resetting the alarm system, and the emotional immune system impacting regulation.
- The gaining of skills and practice
- Life skills, including sleep, nutrition, exercise, relaxation and play etc.
- Boundaries-considering safety rather than control, learning to say no, assertiveness.
- Relationships and balance between codependence and being independent.
- The role of shame
- Target problem areas including self-medication, substance abuse, sexual functioning, self-harm
- empathy and compassion to self and others.
- Traumatic loneliness.

Therapeutic standards

- You must be honest and transparent so to counteract secrecy
- Be open so to counteract the sheer nature of abuse reducing the need to second guess.
- Ensure you do not make promises you are unable to keep
- Make the sessions collaborative.
- Be non-judgmental

- Have a genuine interest in helping others
- Be warm and caring.
- Validate their experiences.
- Take a flexible approach within each session.
- Enable clients to have some control over the pacing of the recovery progress
- Never make assumptions.

Creating a safe setting for therapy

- Discuss exit points i.e. where the toilets are, if refreshments are available etc.
- Develop a safe setting that exudes calmness and ensure no loud noises or external distractions
- Ensure that power and control is restored to the client.
- Consider boundaries and this includes the length of the session, contact outside of sessions, the proposed therapy, self-disclosure and confidentiality.
- Pacing should be client-led.
- There should be no pressure to talk
- Discuss the process
- Discuss the starting and ending points
- Secure the foundations of the therapeutic relationship-ensuring consistent and predictable.

These elements may sound common-sensical, but they are especially important for sufferers of trauma. Clients must feel that they can get up and go to the bathroom at any time throughout the session. If they need a drink, they should be able to access one as nervousness can make the mouth dry. Always have plenty of water with refreshments within the session so that the client can help themselves and have tissues handy nearby too.

By revisiting the trauma, the clients can become agitated, distracted, introverted, nauseous, or anxious. If the client needs to stand and walk around, let them do this.

Always remember that any survivor will be terrified of expressing what they have gone through. Don't be fooled if some can regale it easily, this does not mean that the trauma is not buried deep inside. They may be practicing avoidance. Keeping emotions at bay.

Some clients endure the request to talk and experience great discomfort, but they would rather do this than ask for help. Be aware of their personal space, do not distance yourself but do not be intrusive.

Attachment dynamics within the process.

- Control.
- Trust
- Fear of dependency.
- Fear of intimacy.
- Fear of rejection.
- Insecure attachment style approaching avoiding behaviors.

Client and counsellor attachment style

- Boundaries within therapy.
- Being explicit
- Confidentiality.
- Discussing therapy duration and length of session
- Discussing out of session contact
- Discussing touch
- Discussing self-disclosure

Therapy duration.

Recovery from deeply rooted traumas will take time and only a limited amount of progress can occur in one session. Each client's needs will vary. Most clients would benefit from two years of psychological support as a minimum. It is so important that you assess whether you can commit to such long-term therapy sessions.

You will need resilience and stamina to manage this level of in-depth therapeutic work and your client may need more than one session per week, as such, they will also need to assess whether they can commit to this. The length of the session also needs to be discussed.

Consider that your clients are going to vary when it comes to their ability to remain focused throughout. Some may be able to concentrate for ten or fifteen minutes; others may manage thirty to forty minutes. Others will need longer session times – perhaps an hour and a half. Always consider this fully during the initial assessment. State what would be most beneficial for that client. You must balance the needs of the individual with what you are able to give to them in a professional capacity. The agreed length of the session should be discussed with the client and be a part of the contract.

Contact out of session

Some of your clients are likely to benefit from telephone support in between sessions and this is something you need to consider. Some counsellors provide times when clients can call in and will give additional psychological support, but this must be discussed in advance re frequency, availability and length. They must be focused on helping the clients to develop their grounding skills while also affecting regulation.

It is also worth considering how you would manage chance meetings outside of the therapy sessions and you also need to be clear that you cannot enter any dual relationship and explain why.

Any physical contact between you and your clients must be discouraged. This is especially important when you are working with clients who have experienced such complex traumas. While some counsellors may use touch within the therapeutic setting, it should not be used without considerable thought, or without the evaluation of the benefits or negative aspects of doing so.

Self-disclosure

An element of self-disclosure is warranted. When you are working with survivors of sexual abuse, always be transparent and authentic. It is best to avoid hiding behind the facade of professionalism and to be authentic in your responses. Any self-disclosure should be brief and only in the interest of the client and it must not be used to take the focus away from the client.

Pacing

We have mentioned this before, but it is important. Pacing of the recovery process is crucial because you do not want clients to rush into the whole trauma narrative before they've acquired the skills to manage their reactions. It is true that clients will often push to work through these experiences, and this is because they would have wanted to hurry through the abusive process when it was happening.

When rushing this, it does not allow the potential to reflect upon or process feelings. It also negates understanding. This is why survivors must acquire the relevant skills to be able to manage their responses when exploring their experiences because otherwise it would re-traumatize them. This is why it is important to let the client lead the way when it comes to pacing.

Some clients will automatically start the session when they arrive while others need to relax into the process. Be intuitive and give them the time they need.

Usually, your clients are likely to want a little time when they arrive so to settle in. Part of this can be their hesitance to get started or, to check you are still that secure presence perhaps checking that you are fully available for them. Do respect the settling in process. Do not pressure them to talk. You must also pace the end of the session. Your clients may need a little time to prepare to leave and this is important if the client has brought up very painful memories or feelings – this is likely to be the case if the client has dissociated.

Try to dedicate the last 10 minutes of each session to containing the client and this enables them to manage that transition between the therapeutic setting and the change of environment, so they are ready to embrace the outside world.

Stages of trauma therapy

Stage one

You must establish safety and control within the sessions. Introduce psychoeducation helping the client to develop the necessary skills so to manage their symptoms and to improve their day-to-day functioning. Look at their support network and include the building of your therapeutic relationship.

Stage two

This step includes the processing of the trauma narrative, including traumatic experiences and memories and interconnected abuse dynamics which includes feelings of loss or mourning. It can also include their challenging any distorted core beliefs which would lead to the restoration of reality, enabling grief or mourning is necessary.

Stage three

This enables the client to reconnect to self and enables post-traumatic growth, leading to increased energy and vitality and improved engagement with the world around them.

Module Five

Self-Assessment Task

Task:

A client is struggling to open up and talk within the session, how do you proceed?

Task:

What are open questions and why do you use them?

Task:

Why might a client be able to recount the traumatic events without seeming to be affected?

Please note that these self-assessment tasks are to ensure your understanding of the information within each module. As such, do not submit them for review with Karen E. Wells.

Module Six

The Recovery Process

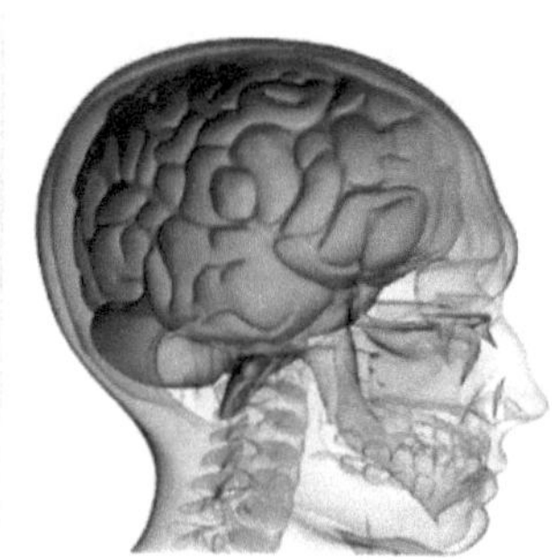

It is easy to see that with such complex issues, the recovery process will be difficult at times and even, arduous. There will be many obstacles to overcome and these will fit alongside some substantial breakthroughs. Think of progress is being the root of small achievements rather than substantial ones. It can take a long time for clients to start feeling more in control and it is wise to expect progress to fluctuate. This is quite normal. Importantly, the client must start to take ownership of their recovery and when they do so, this can be highly rewarding as they feel more in control. To get to this point, you are likely to need a great deal of patience, hope and commitment.

One very useful way to help them take back control of the recovery process is for them to create a symbol that would represent the healing process in action.

Exercise

When you think that a client is ready, discuss them creating a symbol that relates to their recovery progress. It should include any setbacks as well as achievements. They must also consider obstacles yet to face. If they are unsure, you can prompt them to visualize a journey which would include clear, straight routes and yet, there may be difficult terrain to cross. When using metaphors, try to choose ones that relate to something familiar, or to their interests or hobbies. This could be DIY or, it might be that they find cleaning therapeutic, perhaps there is a cupboard that is full to overflowing and clearing it out within the visualization, signifies, clearing the mind from trauma.

Another useful metaphor is their visualizing a protector of self - perhaps a warrior, this might be an image of protection and who fights for them in their hour of need. This is a useful one because it denotes inner strength.

When using the warrior metaphor, you can set up a series of exercises to help them take the next step on their journey to recovery.

Encourage your clients to visualize and access their inner warrior and to write down in list format how they will have helped protect them. This helps them to get in touch with their inner strength and coping strategies. Once they have finished, ask them to consider their list and then discuss how these can be built upon.

It's also important that your clients build a list pertaining to their support network. In some cases, they may not have many people who can provide support to them, but the list can include family and friends. In addition, they can start adding to their support network by including other survivors of trauma. It's useful if they speak to one other survivor or, someone on their support network for five minutes or so each day.

Control combined with a sense of purpose is a positive way to help them recover. Once they can gain some control over their distressing thoughts, or any flashbacks and are able to control their reactions, this will enable them to process their feelings and experiences helping them to be more in control of life on a day-to-day basis.

When they feel more in control, they feel better generally. It empowers them. It can restore sleeping patterns, their desire to eat well and their ability to manage stress levels.

Every step forward should be celebrated, and this can be as simple as tidying the house, or going out shopping alone, or simply playing music and being able to dance or sing along. These are all very normal things, but to a survivor of sexual trauma, this can be a huge step forward.

The focus and whole purpose in recovering from these traumatic experiences will be to regain and improve the quality of life.

So, by restoring some meaning to their lives, this allows them to be more energized, and to live in a way that suits their needs. It's useful to set personal, meaningful goals and to make sure that they are not only realistic but are achievable and measurable too. If the client comes up with a set of goals, it is vital to check that the client's progress will not be restricted by time or financial limitations.

Exercise

We mentioned the use of a journal previously and it can be beneficial for the client to write down all their meaningful goals in the journal and then to prioritize them in order. It can help if you work through the list with them, highlighting the goals that they should focus on immediately and then starting with the number one goal, asked them to identify each step that would be needed so they can attain this goal.

You can also highlight steps that they have already taken and then, list those that come next. Once the goals have been identified, break them down into small manageable steps i.e. think steppingstones as this can make any goal more simplistic. Ask them what steps they can take starting that day so to achieve the goal.

Always remember that the client must work at their own pace and you are there as a support so that they can work through each step until they achieve it. They must validate each step accomplished and record their accomplishments so to be able to look back and chart their progress. Some goals may not be easy to achieve, and they may have to develop workarounds so that they can gradually reach that point. It's important that they try different methods so that they find the right route to achieving success. If a goal or task is too difficult or perhaps, places too much pressure on the client, let them know that they can stop and take a step back from it, but make a firm commitment to return to that point.

Steppingstones enables them to take a measured approach to change and to consider things in a different way while celebrating their achievements, however small. Relishing successes are so important for progress. Small steps create a longer lasting positive experience. If you see clients trying to rush this through, explain why it is better for the clients to take more measured steps. While they are in control of pace, they need to understand the reasons for learning, absorbing and changing. By slowing down, it reduces the cues associated with trauma and enables the mind and the body to have a little more time so to incorporate new ways of being.

Exercise

Another exercise that is useful to help your clients celebrate their achievements, big or small, is for them to write down positive things about themselves on small strips of paper. This should include compliments that they have received, or their accomplishments so far. Then they find a nice container and roll each strip into a ball and place in the container.

If they ever feel the need to reward themselves or to remind themselves of the positive things in their lives, they can take out one of the balls of paper and read it out loud. This reinforces their progress. Equally, they can have an achievement page in their journal, or they can convert a box into an achievement box, and this works the same way.

Surviving survival mode

Your clients may have spent a long time in survival mode, which means that they are constantly on the lookout for danger and will often focus too much on all the negative aspects of the world and the threats they perceive around them. When they are in this mode, it simply leaves very little positive time or space in their minds to focus on all the positive aspects of life. You will gradually start to see them become more positive once control becomes theirs again and then they can move on gradually from being in survival mode.

Meditation and the use of affirmations here can also be extremely useful. It enables them to create space in their minds and to draw in positive energy. This enables greater balance of negative and positive experiences. As the recovery process continues, you will notice that the clients are starting to live fully rather than going into survival mode. This creates greater energy for them so that they can bring more pleasurable activities into life. By doing so, this promotes inner growth.

They also need to learn how to counterbalance traumatic experiences and they can do this by implementing more pleasurable activities. An easy way to replace the negative triggers is to replace them with positive cues instead. One example would be if sexual abuse took place in a silent room, the client may find that the silence makes them unnerved so they can put the radio on or the TV on instead or, play music.

Exercise

When the client is ready, they can start to reflect on the whole abusive experience and with your guidance, identify any triggers that were associated with that time. They need to list some of the more powerful triggers such as silence, light or dark or any associated sense. Link these triggers to mood and their sense of well-being. As they write them down, bearing in mind that this may be difficult for them, start to also list opposing sensory cues and link to them to experiment with these.

If your client was restrained during the sexual abuse, they may have found that feelings of panic and the vulnerability of their situation would make it difficult for them to breathe properly. When they feel anxious, the breath tightens and restricts again. Use breathing techniques to calm them. They can also open windows to calm the sense of panic allowing fresh air to come in. This small step can have considerable benefits. They need to monitor and record how they feel afterwards.

The changing of sensory cues can be done one at a time and some will be more beneficial than others. Once they replace these negative cues with those that are more positive, this should immediately start to lift their sense of well-being and help the recovery process. They can do this by re-claiming their sense of pleasure, too. Often, someone who is abused later in life may have experienced abuse of sorts when younger, but this is not always the case. A child may have been told to stay quiet and not be able to express themselves freely and they may find that being quiet as an adult makes them feel restricted. So, dancing around, or being able to shout or sing, can be empowering. When you are dealing with abuse, there are often many layers to explore. They need to find a way out of those dark times and to develop positive cues.

Once your clients start to feel less overwhelmed and governed by the past, it will gradually feel less threatening. As such, they will start to release any deeply rooted traumas and trapped energy within. Once this energy is released and renewed they can put it towards enjoyable physical activities. This also renews their vitality which enables them to wake up feeling more positive about the day ahead rather than dreading it.

When your clients start to develop control in their lives, they can start to write their own life scripts going forward. Using the metaphor of a book, it can be easy to suggest to your client that they can throw away those earlier chapters (the bad memories) rewrite the chapters or change the outcome of any future ones. If they think that they are the author of their own lives, this enables them to have as much control as they want.

Exercise

Another useful exercise to help your clients redevelop their sense self and to take on more control in their lives, is for them to write down how they feel that their life would have been if they had not experienced the abuse. They need to turn their minds back to any values, hopes and dreams that they would have had before that time.

It's important to remind them that these hopes and dreams and aspirations were stolen from them but that they can now be reclaimed, and this is the next step of their recovery. Discuss the list with them and compare it alongside their goals. They need to make a second list, and prioritize in order of importance, so that they can choose what they wish to reclaim going forward.

Exercise

Another way to fast forward progress but in a natural way is to write down all the things that they are grateful for. They can make notes in their journal detailing the good things in life which might include gratitude for:

- A sunny day
- Personal health
- Health of family and friends
- Nourishing food etc.

Taking this a step forward, they can also write a gratitude letter to someone who is important to them. This person does not need to be alive but, they must have had an important role in their life previously. Practicing gratitude is beneficial because suddenly the small things in life become more important. It could be a moment of happiness, something going well, being able to sleep all night without nightmares…..

Practicing gratitude enables a balance in life reminding the individual of the positive elements to be highlighted.

There's no doubt that change is difficult at first because it means giving up and releasing deeply rooted thought patterns and behaviors too. Habits become so deeply ingrained within, that it can be difficult to imagine finding an alternative way of being. This is even more true for those sufferers of sexual abuse as their reactions to stimuli is very much automatic. In fact, they often occur without any type of conscious awareness at all. Some clients may feel frozen inside and gradually, they must acclimatize to change. Eventually, with guidance, their fearfulness becomes less intense as they process all that has happened.

There is no doubt that obstacles of life are often deeply rooted within the heart of them and so, any specific anxieties or concerns must be addressed one step at a time.

Exercise

Facing fears is something that we are all must do in life but when your clients fear recovery and change this can be terrifying. Each person will have their specific anxieties and while some of your clients will welcome the opportunity to be able to change their lives, others will hold back because they are rigid with fear. This is quite normal. Just let your client acknowledge their fears so they can be discussed.

Ask your clients to make a list of all their worries and fears. The list may be extensive, but that doesn't matter. Just remind them they are in a safe environment and by writing them down, it is easier to overcome them. The fears may focus around a dread of re-experiencing the trauma, or they may be fearful that they cannot stop self-medicating or worrying how change might affect their day-to-day lives.

It is useful for them to also extend this and to write down how they can numb any thoughts and feelings or emotions along with whether they turn to alcohol to help them cope or, they comfort eat etc. They should list this against potential obstacles to recovery. Once the obstacles have been identified, it is possible to discuss solutions. From this, a plan of action can be created.

Note: often obstacles against change include their inner fears or unmanageable emotions. Inner fears trigger that inner alarm system leading to even more anxiety.

Following change, some clients will start to slip back into old patterns of avoidance, and this is usually due to fear. Be open as to why this may be happening. If you see a spiral of fear, it's good to discourage it by addressing it, and bringing their awareness to it. Take them back to previous steppingstones and reset them and by doing so, this gets them back on track.

Make no mistake, fear can be so overwhelming that it can halt that person's progress.

Always remind clients that they can soothe these anxieties through deep breathing techniques and by meditating. This is because fear and anxiety can prevent clear thinking and meditation and deep breathing techniques create clarity and calms too. The clearer their thinking, the easier it will be to make positive decisions rather than reactivating automatic defensive reactions. If the client cannot move beyond the sense of overwhelm and fear, these anxieties can lead to self-fulfilling prophecies.

Secondary trauma is also linked heavily to sexual abuse.

You may find that some of your clients fear they are physically damaged, and these wounds or scars cannot be healed. They may worry that they cannot have children as a result or that no one will want them again. Equally, there can be a deep sense of loneliness that can't be soothed, or their abandonment issues can become so intense that they cannot entertain the thought of letting someone into their life in case it happens again.

Know that all these issues can be worked through and overcome during therapy. Equally, those clients who are still experiencing nightmares, or flashbacks, know that this can impact their energy levels and, prevent additional obstacles to recovery. Beneficial ways to cope with these issues is to focus on the positive elements of life – developing healthy eating patterns, while reducing the amount of caffeine, alcohol, sugar intake. This will naturally enable them to increase their own vitality in life. They should also take action to improve their day to day routines and making sure there are rest times and that they focus when working but also, enable social times too.

Some of your clients will feel very angry and this can prevent them from moving on. They're likely to feel angry with their abuser, and perhaps, even those around them or, if the case went to court, they may be angry with the criminal justice system. Anger is a natural emotion, but it can be toxic if left unchecked. Monitor your clients to see if they are holding back this inner angst and help them to release it. Finding healthy ways to release anger is extremely beneficial. Releasing anger is the absolute first step towards becoming free from this toxic energy.

Deeply rooted feelings of shame or guilt can also create obstacles, especially if the client feels responsible for the abuse happening.

Guilt and self-blame are common.

It happens far more than most people realize. These negative feelings stop them from moving on. It often happens if the abuse has not been fully acknowledged by family members, friends or, the justice system.

Where self-blame exists, it simply reinforces those feelings of shame. Another thing that reinforces feelings of shame is if the individual experiences some pleasurable sensations during the abuse or if they tried to gain comfort from the abuser afterwards. Explain that it is perfectly normal to gain some pleasurable sensations during sexual contact and even if they did not want sex, the brain has a way of protecting them. When you take emotions away from the act, the body can still respond to touch. Even if they tried to seek contact with the abuser afterwards, it does not mean they deserved to be sexually abused. These are a tangle of emotions that can be difficult to break, but it is important that you work through this with them.

Self-worth is often impacted because they believe that they are now damaged goods, and this makes them feel that they do not deserve better treatment in life.

It's important in these cases to consider any negative self-talk that is occurring. Negative mind chatter is all too common and happens subconsciously but when negative thoughts can be captured in the conscious mind, it is possible to change them. Negative self-talk is highly damaging.

Exercise

It's important that the client identifies any negative self-talk and lists any negative messages that they are telling themselves. This may include their not being worthy or that they caused the sexual abuse to happen.

Once they've written the list of any negative messages, they should read these out loud and then become mindful of any emotions or sensations within that occur in direct response to their critical statement. Moving on from this, they need to summon up positive or comforting thoughts about themselves and say these out loud. They then need to reflect as to how that feels. There is likely to be a notable difference. Focus just on these feelings and expand them. Each time they think something negative, they balance it with positive thoughts, and this becomes a new positive habit. It takes time for positive self-talk to become the norm, but it does aid balance and helps them to see that they are damaging themselves.

Module Six

Self-Assessment Tasks

Task:

Try out some of the exercises in this module so to become familiar with using these in a client setting.

Please note that these self-assessment tasks are to ensure your understanding of the information within each module. As such, do not submit them for review with Karen E. Wells.

Final Test

Congratulations on completing this course, we hope you have found it informative and interesting. Please take the time to complete the following assignments and send to kew@kewsolutions

Please allow two months from the completion of this course to provide the following:

1. Write an essay explaining why you wish to be a counsellor in this area of expertise.
2. Write a paragraph specifying one aspect of this course that you found the most surprising.
3. Which aspect of this course was the most difficult to learn?
4. Create a theoretical case study specifying someone who has experienced sexual abuse and how it affected him or her. Discuss how you would treat this person and create a plan of action. This should be 1000 words minimum.

Please send all completed tasks together to the above email address.

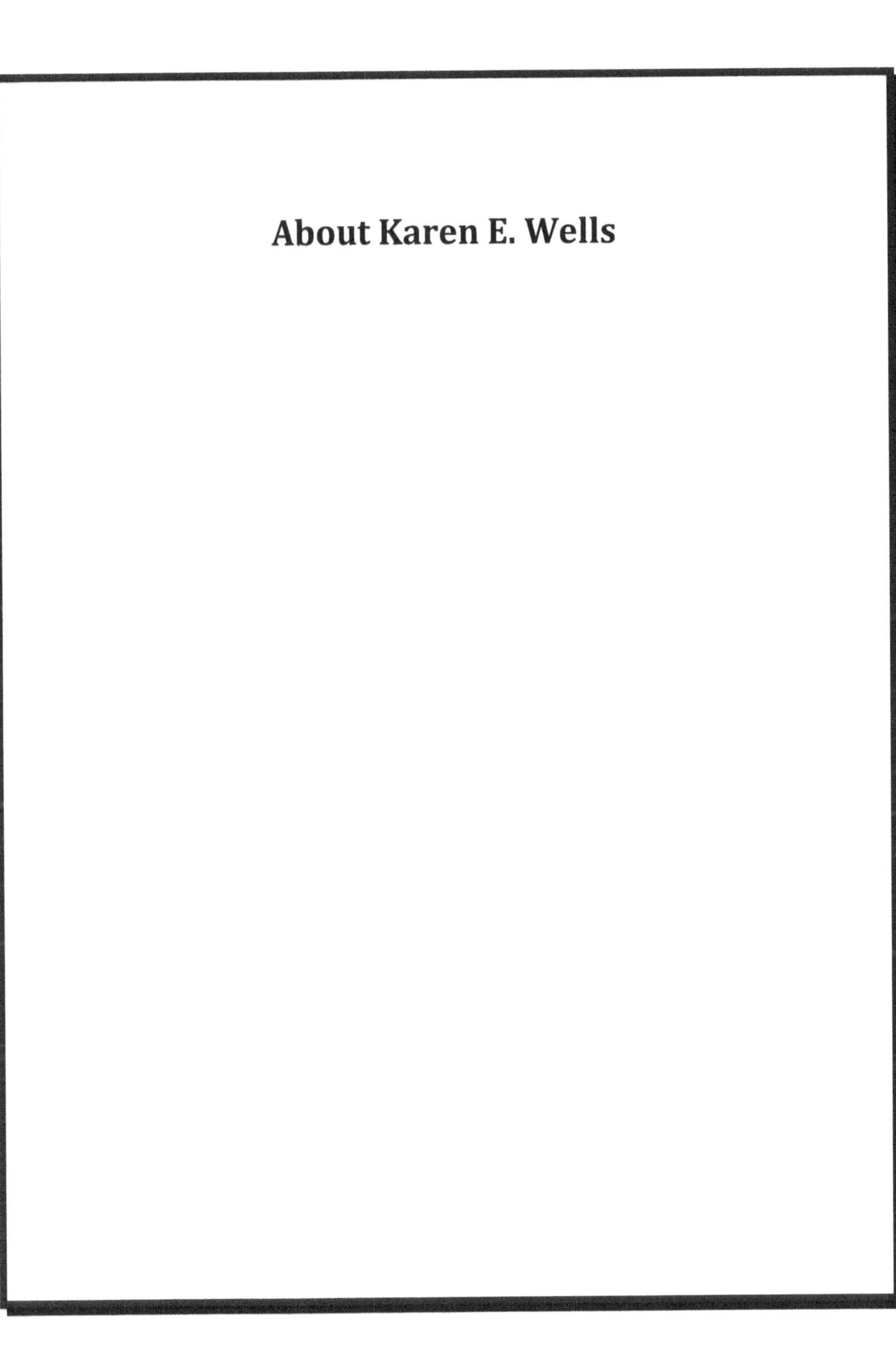

About Karen E. Wells

Professional Counselling
Diploma
for
Sexual Abuse

Karen E. Wells